DRIVE Your Destiny

Jeremiah Chin

HILLSHIRE
—MEDIA—

Address: 15500 VOSS RD, SUITE 586, Sugar Land, TX 77498, United States

TABLE OF CONTENTS

DEDICATION

To my beloved daughters, Elaine and Heidi, and my precious grandson. To Elaine and my grandson Maurice, whose courage during uncertain times has been a beacon of Resilience and Hope, and to Heidi, who faced her challenges alone in Canada. You inspire me to persevere and to complete this book.

To my dear mother, whose spirit remains with me; though we could not be together in her final moments during such difficult times, her love continues to guide me.

This book is a testament to the strength found in adversity, birthed from a time of fear, doubt, and frustration. May it inspire others to embrace their Destiny, even amidst the storms of life.

GENESIS OF
DRIVE YOUR DESTINY

Four years ago, as the world grappled with the uncertainties and upheavals of the COVID-19 pandemic, I found myself on a journey of introspection and reflection. The chaos of those early days forced many of us to reevaluate our lives, values, and dreams. In the midst of this turmoil, the seeds of DRIVE Your Destiny" began to take root.

What started as a response to the global crisis quickly transformed into a profoundly personal exploration of what it means to live a fulfilled life. I poured my thoughts, doubts, and aspirations into this work, wrestling with the themes that would serve as the book's backbone.

The pandemic illuminated the fragility of our existence and the importance of pursuing our true passions. As I wrote, I drew inspiration from the collective struggle, the Resilience of the human spirit, and the profound connections I witnessed in communities striving to uplift one another. Each word became a testament to the power of self-discovery, encouraging readers to embrace their unique paths even when faced with adversity.

Completing this book today feels like a significant achievement for me and everyone who has navigated these challenging years. It serves as a reminder that even in the darkest times, we can shape our destinies. The lessons shared within these pages are rooted in my belief that purpose and fulfillment are attainable for all of us—if we dare to pursue our dreams, confront our fears, and stay true to our values.

I invite you to embark on this journey of self-exploration and empowerment. May "DRIVE Your Destiny" inspire you to reclaim your narrative, awaken your passions, and steer your life toward a future filled with purpose and joy.

Join me as we embrace the power within us to drive forward into the unknown, knowing that our destinies are ours to shape.

Your Heart and Health Mentor,

Jeremiah Chin

D.R.I.V.E. And many more.

Skills for workplace longevity and enhancing your personal career journey.

Boost your professional longevity with DRIVE.

INTRODUCTION

This book is written during a massive and challenging global pandemic: COVID-19.

Imagine the profound impact COVID-19 has had on our lives and livelihoods. With approximately 2.6 billion people under some form of lockdown, many are experiencing the toxic effects of extended isolation. There has been a rise in child abuse, increased fights and quarrels among siblings, and a spike in divorce rates. Moreover, we must consider the mental toll and stress that many are enduring. The quarantine has imposed a significant psychological impact on numerous lives, leaving many devastated. We are witnessing anxiety, anger, mood swings, depression, and even suicides at an alarming rate worldwide. This is the kind of invisible warfare the world faces today without the firing of a single missile.

The dilemma of prioritizing lives and livelihoods—whether to prioritize safety or reopen the economy—poses a significant global challenge for policymakers. It reminds me of a game we used to play: trying to knock your opponent off a pole splattered with oil. But this time, we must try to hold onto each other on a pole greased with oil, which is incredibly tough. That's precisely what COVID-19 is doing to the world. Countries that were previously shut down are opening up, only to face the disheartening reality of second waves or resurgences of the virus. If Singapore doesn't open up quickly, more shops will close, more jobs will be lost, and more people will suffer the consequences of this tragic situation.

Consider what happens when you operate within the constraints of the world's economy or structure: You spend 20 years of your life in school and over 40 years in the workforce, striving to enjoy the last third of your life in old age—some with aches and pains, albeit some are more fortunate than others. Yet, the majority of Singaporeans are facing significant challenges. This is the life we have been conditioned to live—"work until you die."

COVID-19 has become the fastest disruptor of change, representing a paradigm shift at its most extreme—sudden, unexpected, and deadly.

For many, retrenchment, early retirement, and total shutdown have become harsh realities. With the government subsidy package ending this month, what does the next five months and beyond hold for the ordinary Singaporean?

Our government is navigating a difficult task, juggling numerous challenges simultaneously. We must be grateful for a government that is level-headed enough to work through this crisis. It is essential that we do our part to ensure we keep this invisible enemy at bay. How long will this pandemic last?

The unfortunate truth is that we do not know.

Post note: Moving forward into 2025, even with the entrance of the Trump Administration, it is still too early to anticipate what kind of influence it will have on the world. The Trump administration significantly shaped the global landscape across different domains like the economy, healthcare, and social issues, just to name a few.

During times like these, we need to think outside the box and approach things differently. We need to reignite our inner DRIVE, discover our true-life purpose, set our Direction amidst multiple uncertainties, and chart a course to reach our Destiny.

This is what this book is about:

DRIVE to Destiny.

Starting out: Ready Fire Aim

If you don't have a DRIVE, you may find yourself lost forever.

Have you seen a dog chasing its tail?

There's a lot of activity, but it remains in the same place. What about a rocking chair?

It moves back and forth, yet it isn't going anywhere.

Who are you, and what are you looking for in life?

Many individuals navigate their life's journey without understanding what they want or how to get there. Not knowing the "WHAT," "HOW," and "WHERE" is not as problematic as not knowing the "WHY."

I'm here to hold your steering wheel and help you drive through this journey together. Are you with me? Ready Aim

So let's DRIVE.

D.R.I.V.E. is an acronym.

IT STARTS WITH A DREAM.

Do you have a dream? What is it? Why is this important to you? If you don't know your "WHY," you may find yourself living a nightmare down the road. The long and winding road of life is often anything but smooth. Sometimes, you hit a pothole; other times, you encounter bottlenecks and traffic jams. Your dream must be measured by its outcome. What do you truly want? Are the choices you are making now in alignment with your dream, or are they sabotaging your life at every turn? Your success hinges on your preferences.

What would you choose to do if money were no concern and you had infinite time until your dying day? Reflect for a moment: what was your childhood dream?

I cannot help but recall the famous speech by Martin Luther King Jr. And this is how he started his speech:

"I HAVE A DREAM...' so you see, everything starts with a dream. Your DREAM.

Finding and nurturing your dreams can be a lifeline to a fulfilling life, offering purpose, motivation, and a sense of joy. Here's what you can do:

1. Do some self-reflection and exploration. Identify what interests you. Try new things. Don't be afraid to step outside your comfort zone and explore…Connect with people passionate about things you admire and learn from their experience.

2. Turn your DREAM into a passion. Set a realistic goal by breaking down your goals into smaller achievable steps to stay motivated and on track. And don't be afraid to fail.

"Follow your passion, be prepared to work hard and sacrifice, and above all, don't let anyone limit your dreams."

- Donovan Bailey

Then there are the inevitable roadblocks you didn't expect— like the one we were navigating: COVID-19.

Just imagine. In Singapore alone, 8,663 businesses closed their doors in April 2020. The nation's GDP was expected to shrink between 4% and 7% as the growth forecast was revised downward due to the impact of the pandemic.

Familiar names like JC Penney, Gold's Gym, and GNC have fallen into decline, illustrating the harsh realities of this global crisis. Even fashion retailers are shutting down and are unable to adapt to online delivery mechanisms. We faced this grim reality, characterized by job losses and retrenchments.

What did the future hold if the situation did not improve?

Was there a way out of this crisis?

Could we derive the best from the worst situation during this pandemic?

Fortunately, there are ways forward.

The big WHY

First and foremost, understand your big **"WHY."** The bigger your "WHY," the better it will ground you or risk drowning you. Four years ago, we lived as if the world would not change. Suddenly, however, the temperature has risen, and the global fever is at an all-time high—devastating, in fact.

Aviation industries have been grounded. Establishments in food and beverage have had their clientele disappear.

Tourists have lost the ability to travel. Convention centers, cinemas, and conferences have fallen silent, replaced by staring contests at home—at the walls, the computer, the TV, or with our pets.

What happens over the next few months is crucial. Some will be forced into early retirement or become victims of unfortunate retrenchments.

Yes, the world has changed. Work and home are beginning to intertwine, representing the future of living. You will require new skill sets to thrive—or, in some cases, merely to survive.

So, what is it going to be for you?

Is your cup half full, or is it half empty?

Your answer to this question is crucial.

Why? Because your primary "WHY" may evoke deep emotions, while your secondary "WHY" will empower you to DRIVE forward. That's why.

Post note: These principles, concepts, and values are independent of space and time; therefore, they are applicable in every situation.

D STANDS FOR DESIRE.

You are the DRIVER of your life.

What do you aspire to BE?

We are born first to 'be' and then to 'do.' That's why we identify as human beings rather than 'human doings.' Earning a living is essential. Achieving success is commendable. Attaining fame in your pursuits can be gratifying.

However, your aspirations must transcend these surface-level goals if your life is to be enriched with meaning and fulfillment. Life is not merely about eating, drinking, or indulging in merriment. The COVID-19 pandemic has highlighted another dimension of life that we often overlook: mental and emotional health.

These dimensions are integral components of our physical existence. While COVID-19 has infected more than 54,000 individuals, the number of people whose mental health has been adversely affected by the pandemic remains uncertain (even in 2025.)

Consider a stool—it has three legs. The stool's stability, steadiness, and solidity depend on all three legs being intact. Remove one leg, and you'll struggle to sit comfortably. Similarly, mental, emotional, and spiritual health are crucial during challenging times like these. Those who face mental health issues need support and encouragement now more than ever. The constraints of confinement exacerbate these problems. Instances of child abuse, arguments between family members, and divorce rates are on the rise.

For those of us coping well, it's essential to practice "other-mindedness"—a mindset that encourages us to think of others and extend our support to those who are vulnerable. With empathy and understanding, we can help lift those who are struggling.

We need to strengthen the emotional, mental, and spiritual support systems around us while pursuing our desires and dreams. Remember, as you embark on this journey of self-discovery and aspiration, you are not alone. We must collectively strive to ensure that while we pursue our goals, we also contribute to the well-being of our communities.

Let's pause here and discuss a few myths surrounding Money, Fame, and Success.

These three elusive words carry different meanings for different people. What is your perspective on this? How do you define these three concepts?

The story we often hear regarding success hasn't changed much over the years: "Be good, study hard, get good grades, attend a reputable university, excel in your field, secure a well-paying job, climb the corporate ladder, save money, get married, raise a family, do your best until retirement, and then enjoy life." This narrative perpetuates the cycle as we tell our children the same things.

"You are rich, you are successful, and you are happy now," we say.

"But Papa, you don't look happy," the child might respond.

This perfectly illustrates the disconnect. Wealth, success, and happiness are defined by who a person IS, not merely by what they HAVE. While your bank account may suggest otherwise, a person's true worth cannot be measured solely through the lens of material wealth, especially in the eyes of a higher power. The relentless pursuit of wealth, fame, and happiness as ends in themselves resembles a futile chase after your own shadow. The world is filled with evidence and examples of individuals who have succumbed to this lie. Many have fallen prey to the notion that these surface-level achievements equate to a meaningful life.

The tragedy of suicide affects individuals from all walks of life, including those who are rich and famous. Here are a few notable examples of celebrities who tragically took their own lives despite their success and fame:

1. Robin Williams (1951-2014) The beloved actor and comedian, known for his roles in films like "Good Will Hunting" and "Mrs. Doubtfire," battled severe depression and anxiety. His unexpected death by suicide shocked fans around the world and highlighted the importance of mental health awareness.

2. Kate Spade (1962-2018) - The renowned fashion designer and entrepreneur known for her handbags and accessories struggled with depression. Her death brought attention to mental health issues and the often-hidden challenges faced by those in the public eye.

3. Anthony Bourdain (1956-2018) - The celebrated chef, author, and television personality was known for his travel and food shows, particularly "Parts Unknown." Bourdain's death by suicide highlighted the complexities of mental health and the pressures faced in the entertainment industry.

*4. **Kurt Cobain (1967-1994)** - The lead singer of the influential band Nirvana, Cobain became a symbol of the grunge movement. His struggles with fame, mental health, and substance abuse ultimately led to his suicide, raising awareness about the dark side of celebrity.*

*5. **Virginia Woolf (1882-1941)** - Though primarily recognized as a literary figure rather than a celebrity in the modern sense, Woolf was a prominent writer and intellectual. She struggled with mental illness throughout her life and died by suicide, leaving a profound legacy in literature and discussions surrounding mental health.*

These tragic cases remind us that mental health issues can affect anyone, regardless of their successes or public personas. It's important to foster understanding and support for those who may be struggling.

Consider this carefully:

When you navigate life according to the world's economy or structure, this is what you typically encounter: You invest 20 years in education and expend over 40 years working to eventually enjoy the last third of your life in retirement—some fortunate enough to do so with minimal discomfort.

In contrast, others suffer from lingering aches and pains. Yet, the stark reality is that many Singaporeans face significant challenges. We are conditioned to embrace this mentality: a "work till you die" philosophy.

But is this the life you truly desire?

Let's redefine what success means to you. Perhaps it's time to go beyond conventional definitions and explore a more fulfilling path that represents true wealth, authentic success, and genuine happiness.

Take a moment to reflect: *What do these three concepts mean to you? Are they merely markers of status, or do they embody deeper values that resonate with your purpose?*

The traditional narrative tells us to follow a well-trodden path, ensuring we secure a respectable job, make a good living, and retire comfortably. Yet, this formula leaves many people feeling unfulfilled and disconnected. The truth is that achieving such milestones does not inherently guarantee happiness or contentment.

Instead, we must cultivate a mindset recognizing the importance of inner wealth, personal growth, emotional intelligence, and relationships with others. True success lies in the richness of our experiences and connections rather than the digits in our bank accounts.

The pandemic has exposed the fragility of our constructed realities, prompting us to reconsider our priorities. Are we merely existing within the frameworks set by society, or are we proactively crafting lives that reflect our true passions and desires?

As we step into an uncertain future, it is crucial to remember that we have the power to redefine what it means to live a meaningful life. Perhaps it's time to challenge the myths surrounding money, fame, and success and to seek fulfillment in ways that resonate with our authentic selves.

Let's embark on this journey together, redefining our goals and aspirations in a world that, while shaken, still brims with potential for those who dare to dream beyond the conventional.

So, who doesn't want to be happy? Raise your hand.

Everyone desires happiness.

But here's the truth: Poor people die, and so do rich, famous, and successful individuals. In this regard, we are all equal. Many impoverished individuals pass away feeling unhappy, yet just as many wealthy, renowned, and supposedly successful individuals leave this world in discontent.

Why is this the case? This brings us back to the BIG WHY. Why is understanding your "WHY" so important?

Grasping your **"WHY"** can either anchor you or drag you under. It serves as a compass guiding your decisions, aspirations, and life's Direction, especially during turbulent times. When you have a clear sense of purpose—your own "WHY"—you can navigate the storms of life with Resilience.

Consider what truly fulfills you. Is it the constant chase after external validation in the form of wealth and fame, or is it the intrinsic joys found in meaningful relationships, personal growth, and making a positive impact in the lives of others?

As we reflect on our journey, let us dare to ask ourselves: Are we merely existing to meet societal expectations, or are we consciously choosing to pursue a purpose that resonates with our core values? True fulfillment arises from aligning our daily actions with our deeper aspirations rather than conforming to a predetermined narrative imposed by society.

Finding happiness isn't solely about accumulating wealth, recognition, or status—it's about living authentically and intentionally. So, seek out your "WHY." Understand that while we all aspire to be happy, it is crucial to define what happiness means to you.

Together, let's embark on this journey of discovery to redefine success, prioritize well-being, and drive towards a fulfilling life filled with purpose.

The world has repeatedly demonstrated that success, fame, and money cannot buy happiness.

If I could peer into the minds of those who seem to have it all, what do you think I would observe? Perhaps it would be filled with thoughts like, "If only I had…" or "If only I could…" and yet, despite possessing wealth, fame, and success, they died unhappy. So, what could be the reasons behind their unhappiness?

Could it be due to environmental influences? Unfulfilled relationships? They may not be alone in the physical sense, yet they feel profoundly lonely. These individuals, rich, famous, and successful, often experience a lack of true fulfillment. Pursuing riches, fame, and success is akin to putting the cart before the horse.

Instead of driving their lives forward, they merely push, lacking the control and Direction needed to navigate their journey. You must take the wheel and **DRIVE YOUR DESTINY** with your Head and Heart.

It's vital to understand that there is a distinct difference between destiny and destination. I chose Destiny deliberately because it encompasses much more than just a final stop on your journey.

Your destination might be a particular goal—a job title, a specific annual income, several followers on social media— but destiny is about the journey, the experiences you gather along the way, and the legacy you build. It is the deeper purpose that fills your life with meaning and satisfaction.

When aligned with your Destiny, you are not just chasing after fleeting moments of success but creating a life rich with intention and impact. You must ask yourself: What does my faithful Destiny look like? What makes my Heart sing? What legacy do I want to leave behind?

Taking charge of your Destiny means acknowledging your true aspirations and pursuing them wholeheartedly. It requires introspection, self-awareness, and the courage to embrace your unique path rather than conforming to the expectations set by society.

So, let's shift gears. Let's stop pushing and start driving. Embrace the power within you to steer your life toward genuine fulfillment, purpose, and happiness.

Sometimes, we don't end up where we genuinely want to go when we drive. We fail to reach our desired destination. So, what happened? We often find ourselves saying, "Ah, I'm destined or fated to fail, to be poor, or to remain stuck in this situation.

Too bad. That's just life.

These objections can become deeply ingrained beliefs, acting as a mental barrier to change. Some might say, "**I've worked hard; nothing ever changes.**" Others might argue, "**The system is rigged; it favors those who already have money and connections.**" Many feel trapped in their circumstances, believing they lack the necessary resources or opportunities to redefine their paths. **"What if I try and fail? It's safer not to try at all,"** some think.

Then there are those who are quick to blame external factors: **"The economy is too unstable" or "My job doesn't allow for growth." "I'm too old to start something new. What would my family think?"** These fears and excuses become a comfortable narrative that keeps them from pursuing their true desires.

This skepticism leads to what I like to call the work-life scam. The constant grind of working long hours merely to get by often traps individuals in a cycle of discontent.

What's the point of sacrificing your time and spirit if, at the end of the day, you feel unfulfilled? This scam convinces us that success is synonymous with endless toil, blurring the line between productivity and true purpose.

And that brings us to the next important word…

D STANDS FOR DIRECTION

Do you know where you are going?

Yes, where are you heading in life?

It's crucial to ask yourself these questions regularly. The path you take matters, and without clear direction, you may wander aimlessly.

Here's a lighthearted illustration to consider:

You may have heard the old joke: *"A man is driving down the road when he sees another man standing by the roadside, looking completely lost. The first man stops and asks, 'Where are you going?' To which the lost man responds, 'I don't know!' The first man grins and says, 'Well, then, hop in! I can take you anywhere!'"*

This joke underscores a vital truth:

If you don't have a defined destination, you may end up anywhere—often nowhere productive. Everyone thought **"Anybody"** could achieve their goals, yet **"Nobody"** realized that **"Everybody"** wouldn't commit to the process. In the end, **"Everybody"** blamed **"Somebody"** for the lack of progress, while **"Nobody"** took responsibility. Nothing got accomplished.

It's essential to recognize the importance of taking ownership of your journey. You must be proactive about defining both your desired outcomes and the steps necessary to get there. Clarity of Direction empowers you to steer your life purposefully, preventing you from veering off course into the chaos of complacency or despair.

So, I implore you to take a moment to reflect on your direction.

Ask yourself:

Where am I headed? What truly matters to me?

Begin charting your course toward a life filled with intention, fulfillment, and, most importantly, driving toward your authentic Destiny.

What if I told you that you can win with the cards that are dealt to you?

What if you could find happiness in what you do while feeling fulfilled because you are pursuing your passions for the right reasons?

> *Now, you can place the horse in front of the cart and DRIVE. Don't just push your way through life; engage intentionally and purposefully.*

So, how can we win with the cards we are dealt? The key is to refuse to be a victim of circumstance. Instead, empower yourself! You have the ability to shape your outcomes, regardless of how unfairly or unexpectedly life may unfold.

To help you on this journey, I invite you to take a step forward.

This is what you need to do to prepare you when you step on the gas pedal of your life's journey.

1. Mental Strategies for Clarity and Focus

-Mindfulness Meditation:

Practice being present in the moment to reduce stress and improve focus.

- Journaling:

Write down your thoughts, goals, and reflections to gain clarity and track progress.

- Visualization:

Imagine yourself achieving your goals or living out your values to stay motivated.

2. Mental Strategies for Resilience

- Reframing:

Turn negative thoughts into opportunities for growth (e.g., "This is hard, but I'm learning so much").

- Gratitude Practice:

List three things you're grateful for daily to shift your mindset toward positivity.

- Self-Compassion:

Treat yourself with kindness during setbacks instead of being overly critical.

3. Mental Strategies for Integrity

- Daily Check-Ins:

Ask yourself, "Did my actions today align with my values?"

- Accountability Partners:

Share your goals with someone who can help keep you on track.

- Pause and Reflect:

Before making decisions, take a moment to consider if they align with your principles.

4. Mental Strategies for Vision

- Goal Setting:

Break down your vision into actionable steps and set deadlines.

- Affirmations:

Use positive statements like, I am capable of achieving my dreams to reinforce your belief in your vision.

- Regular Reviews:

Revisit your goals weekly or monthly to ensure you're on track.

5. Mental Strategies for Empathy

- *Active Listening:*

Focus entirely on the speaker without interrupting or judging.

- *Perspective-Taking:*

Imagine yourself in someone else's shoes to better understand their feelings.

- *Kindness Rituals:*

Make it a habit to perform small acts of kindness daily.

6. Mental Strategies for Stress Management

- Breathing Exercises:

Practice deep breathing to calm your mind during stressful moments.

- Time Blocking:

Schedule specific times for work, rest, and self-care to avoid burnout.

- Digital Detox:

Take breaks from screens to recharge mentally.

7. Mental Strategies for Growth Mindset

- *Embrace Challenges:*

View obstacles as opportunities to learn and grow.

- *Celebrate Effort:*

Focus on the process rather than just the outcome.

- *Seek Feedback:*

Ask for constructive criticism to improve and grow.

8. Mental Strategies for Motivation

- Find Your "Why":

Remind yourself of the deeper reason behind your goals.

- Small Wins:

Celebrate small achievements to stay motivated.

- Inspiration Boards:

Create a visual board with images and quotes that inspire you.

"Go confidently in the direction of your dreams. Live the life you have imagined."

. Henry David Thoreau:

Your commitment to personal growth starts here!

This brings us to the next letter: R.

R STANDS FOR READINESS.

Are you ready to let your dreams and desires guide you to where you want to go? It's important to be cautious about what you dream of, as you may not be fully prepared to handle it. To embark on the journey of your life, you must first create a ROADMAP or a BLUEPRINT. But what do you do with this map? Here's a sample:

Readiness—being prepared with a clear blueprint or roadmap—is critical in turning your vision into reality. It ensures that you're not just dreaming about the future but actively working toward it in a structured and intentional way.

Here's why readiness matters and how to create a blueprint or roadmap to guide your journey: ---Why Readiness is Important

Provides Clarity and Direction

A blueprint or roadmap breaks down your vision into actionable steps, making it easier to know what to do next. - Without a plan, it's easy to feel overwhelmed or lost

Keeps You Focused

A clear plan helps you prioritize tasks that align with your vision and avoid distractions. -

Example: If your vision is to start a business, a roadmap ensures you focus on essential steps like market research and funding.

Builds Confidence

Knowing you have a plan in place reduces anxiety and boosts your belief in your ability to succeed.

Example: A student with a study schedule feels more confident about acing an exam.

Enhances Accountability

A roadmap holds you accountable by setting deadlines and milestones.

Example: Tracking progress toward fitness goals keeps you motivated.

Prepares You for Challenges

A well-thought-out plan anticipates potential obstacles and includes strategies to overcome them.

Example: If funding is a challenge for your business, your roadmap might include alternative funding sources.

Maximizes Efficiency

A blueprint ensures you use your time, energy, and resources effectively.

Example: A project manager with a detailed timeline avoids wasted effort and delays.

"How to Create a Blueprint or Roadmap.'

A blueprint or roadmap is a step-by-step plan that outlines how you'll achieve your vision.

Here's how to create one:

Define Your Vision and Goals

Vision: What does your desired future look like? (e.g., "I want to be a successful author.")

Goals: Break your vision into specific, measurable goals. (e.g., "Publish my first novel within 3 years.")

Break Goals into Milestones- Divide your goals into smaller, achievable milestones.

Example:

Goal: Publish a novel.

Milestones:

1. Complete a writing course (Month 1-3).

2. Write the first draft (Month 4-9).

3. Edit the draft (Month 10-12).

4. Query literary agents (Month 13-15).

5. Secure a publishing deal (Month 16-18).

6. Launch the book (Month 19-24).

- Identify Resources and Tools

What do you need to achieve each milestone?

Example: - Writing software, a mentor, a writing group, or funding for editing services.

- Set Deadlines

Assign realistic timelines to each milestone.

 Example: "Finish the first draft by Month 9."

- Anticipate Challenges

Identify potential obstacles and plan how to overcome them.

Example: Challenge: Writer's block.

Solution:

Set a daily writing habit and join a writing group for accountability.

- Track Progress

Regularly review your roadmap to ensure you're on track. –

Example: Use a journal, spreadsheet, or project management tool to track milestones.

- Stay Flexible

Be open to adjusting your plan as you learn and grow.

Example: If you realize self-publishing is a better option, update your roadmap accordingly.

Example Blueprint: Starting a Business.

Vision:

Build a sustainable business that empowers local artisans.

Goals:

Launch the business within 2 years and achieve $100,000 in revenue by Year 3.

Milestones:

1. Research and Planning (Months 1-3)

Study the market and identify target customers.

Create a business plan.

2. Product Development (Months 4-6)

Partner with local artisans to create products.

Test product quality and pricing.

3. Funding (Months 7-9)

Apply for grants or loans. –

Launch a crowdfunding campaign.

4. Branding and Marketing (Months 10-12)

Design a logo and website. - Build a social media presence.

5. Launch (Months 13-15)

Open an online store. - Host a launch event.

6. Growth (Months 16-24)

Expand product lines.

Build partnerships with retailers.

Tips for Staying Ready

- *Review Your Roadmap Regularly*
- *Check your progress weekly or monthly and adjust as needed.*
- *Celebrating Small Wins*
- *Acknowledge achievements to stay motivated.*
- *Stay Organized*
- *Use tools like calendars, to-do lists, or apps to manage tasks.*
- *Seek Feedback –*
- *Share your roadmap with a mentor or trusted friend for input.*
- *Stay Adaptable.*
- *Be prepared to pivot if circumstances change.*

Final Thought

Readiness transforms your vision from a dream into an actionable plan. By creating a blueprint or roadmap, you set yourself up for success, ensuring that every step you take moves you closer to your desired future. Let me know if you'd like to help create a personalized roadmap for your vision!

CHECK.

R STANDS FOR REALITY CHECK

This is a crucial step. In our upcoming Reality Check Workshop, you will engage with various exercises and questionnaires designed to provide clarity about your current circumstances and aspirations.

In order to discover your Personal Drive, we must start with a foundational step:

A. *Self-Assessment Exercise*

The Holland Code (RIASEC) Test is a self-report inventory that measures an individual's interests in six different areas: Realistic, Investigative, Artistic, Social, Enterprising, and Conventional. The test was developed by John L. Holland in the 1950s, and it is based on his theory of personality, which states that individuals are motivated to engage in activities that are consistent with their personality type. The RIASEC Test is widely used in career counseling and research, and it has been shown to be a reliable and valid measure of interests.

The RIASEC model is a six-factor model of personality that was developed by John L. Holland. The six factors are:

- *Realistic (R): Individuals with this personality type are practical and like to work with their hands. They are good at solving problems and working with tools.*
- *Investigative (I): Individuals with this personality type are curious and like to learn new things. They are good at solving problems and working with numbers.*
- *Artistic (A): Individuals with this personality type are creative and like to express themselves through art, music, or writing. They are good at coming up with new ideas and solving problems in new ways.*
- *Social (S): Individuals with this personality type are caring and like to help others. They are good at working with people and resolving conflicts.*
- *Enterprising (E): Individuals with this personality type are outgoing and like to take risks. They are good at leading others and selling things.*
- *Conventional (C): Individuals with this personality type are organized and like to follow rules. They are good at keeping track of details and working with numbers.*

A simple test that you can do for free is this link here: https://openpsychometrics.org

Of course, this is for educational and information purposes only. Seek a professional practitioner for an accurate assessment. Try it.

Below is a sample of what it looks like.

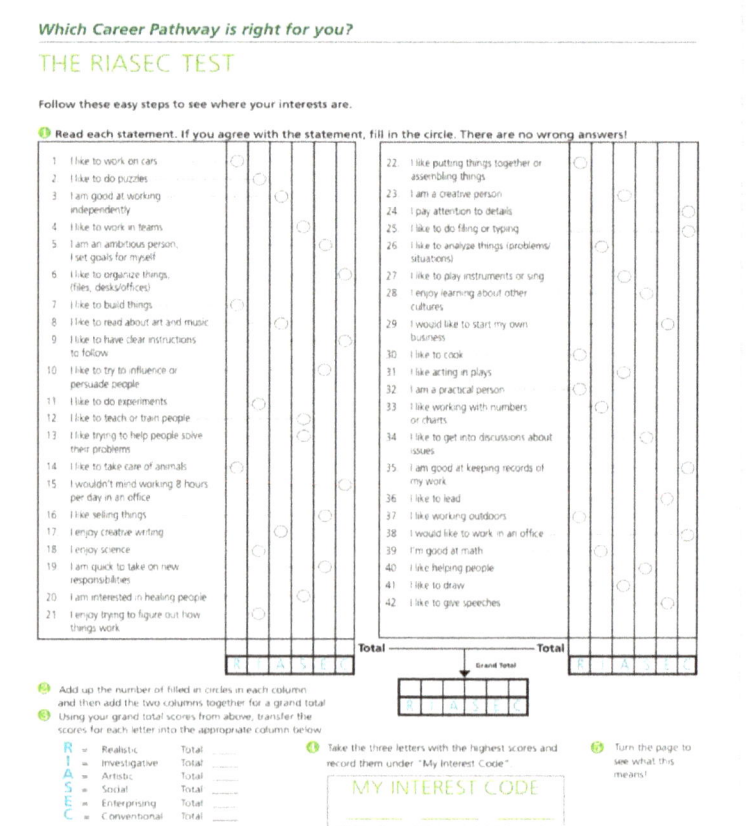

RESULTS OF THE RIASEC TEST

R = Realistic

These people are often good at mechanical or athletic jobs. Good college majors for Realistic people are

- Agriculture
- Health Assistant
- Computers
- Construction
- Mechanic/Machinist
- Engineering
- Food and Hospitality

Related Pathways

Natural Resources

Health Services

Industrial and Engineering Technology

Arts and Communication

I = Investigative

These people like to watch, learn, analyze and solve problems. Good college majors for Investigative people are...

- Marine Biology
- Engineering
- Chemistry
- Zoology
- Medicine/Surgery
- Consumer Economics
- Psychology

Related Pathways

Health Services

Business

Public and Human Services

Industrial and Engineering Technology

A = Artistic

These people like to work in unstructured situations where they can use their creativity. Good majors for Artistic people are

- Communications
- Cosmetology
- Fine and Performing Arts
- Photography
- Radio and TV
- Interior Design
- Architecture

Related Pathways

Public and Human Services

Arts and Communication

S = Social

These people like to work with other people, rather than things. Good college majors for Social people are...

- Counseling
- Nursing
- Physical Therapy
- Travel
- Advertising
- Public Relations
- Education

Related Pathways

Health Services

Public and Human Services

E = Enterprising

These people like to work with others and enjoy persuading and performing. Good college majors for Enterprising people are

- Fashion Merchandising
- Real Estate
- Marketing/Sales
- Law
- Political Science
- International Trade
- Banking/Finance

Related Pathways

Business

Public and Human Services

Arts and Communication

C = Conventional

These people are very detail oriented, organized and like to work with data. Good college majors for Conventional people are ...

- Accounting
- Court Reporting
- Insurance
- Administration
- Medical Records
- Banking
- Data Processing

Related Pathways

Health Services

Business

Industrial and Engineering Technology

So, this is what you need to do.

1. Identify Your Core Values:

Reflect on what truly matters to you. What principles do you want to guide your life? Make a list of your top five core values.

2. Assess Your Strengths and Weaknesses.

What are you good at? What areas require improvement? Be honest with yourself—this is a pivotal moment for growth.

3. Clarify Your Goals.

Write down your short-term and long-term goals. Be specific about what you want to achieve in different areas of your life—career, relationships, health, and personal growth.

4. Examine Your Current Situation:

Evaluate where you are right now in relation to your goals. What are the gaps, and what resources or changes do you need to bridge them?

5. Seek Feedback:

Don't hesitate to ask for input from trusted friends, mentors, or colleagues. Sometimes, others can see things in us that we overlook.

Through this self-assessment, you will gain insight into your current reality and identify the steps needed to progress towards your dreams. Becoming fully aware of your starting point is crucial before planning your next moves.

Remember, the journey to personal fulfillment begins with understanding where you are and where you want to go. So, let's get ready to embrace your dreams and desires, take control of your journey, and ultimately DRIVE toward a future filled with purpose and satisfaction.

Personality Performance Profiling

As part of your self-assessment, it's essential to conduct a SWOT analysis of yourself. This involves evaluating:

*- **Strengths:** What are your innate talents and qualities that stand out?*

*- **Weaknesses:** What areas might require further development?*

*- **Opportunities**: What external opportunities can you seize to enhance your journey?*

*- **Threats**: What challenges do you face that could hinder your progress?*

C. Where is the GAP?

Once we prepare you to BE your authentic self, we must align you with what you love to do. This brings us to the next word: Resilience.

R FOR RESILIENCE

In an era characterized by rapid changes and constant challenges, the concept of Resilience has emerged as a vital trait for individuals seeking to thrive. At its core, Resilience refers to the capacity to recover from difficulties and adapt to challenging circumstances. It is not merely the ability to bounce back but also to harness setbacks as opportunities for growth. In "DRIVE," Resilience, therefore, serves as the backbone for these elements. When individuals encounter obstacles, those who possess Resilience can maintain their motivation and commitment, ultimately enhancing their journey toward mastery and fulfilling their sense of purpose.

Maya Angelou once said: *"You may encounter many defeats, but you must not be defeated. In fact, it may be necessary to encounter defeat so you can know who you are, what you can rise from, and how you can still come out of it."*

Likewise, according to J.K. Rowling: *"Rock bottom became the solid foundation on which I rebuilt my life."*

Here are some simple tips on how to stay Resilient.

Mental Strategies to Stay Strong Through Challenges (Resilience)

1. Reframe Challenges as Opportunities

 - _Shift your mindset by asking, What can I learn from this? Or How can this make me stronger?_

 - _Example: Instead of thinking, This is too hard, try. This is a chance to grow._

2. Practice Gratitude

 - _Write down three things you're grateful for daily, even during tough times._

 - _Gratitude helps shift focus from what's going wrong to what's going right._

3. Develop a Growth Mindset

 - _Believe that challenges are opportunities to improve, not threats to your abilities._

 - _Use affirmations like, I am capable of overcoming this._

4. Break Problems into Smaller Steps

- When faced with a big challenge, break it into manageable tasks.

- Focus on one step at a time to avoid feeling overwhelmed.

5. Lean on Your Support System

- Reach out to friends, family, or mentors for encouragement and advice.

- Sharing your struggles can lighten the emotional load.

6. Practice Self-Compassion

- Treat yourself with kindness, especially when things don't go as planned.

- Remind yourself that setbacks are part of the journey.

7. Visualize Success

- Imagine yourself overcoming the challenge and achieving your goal.

- Visualization can boost confidence and motivation.

8. Stay Present with Mindfulness

 - *Practice mindfulness techniques like deep breathing or meditation to stay grounded.*

 - *Focus on the present moment instead of worrying about the future.*

9. Learn from Past Challenges

 - *Reflect on previous obstacles you've overcome and how you did it.*

 - *Use those experiences as proof that you can handle this one, too.*

10. Celebrate Small Wins

 - *Acknowledge and celebrate progress, no matter how small.*

 - *This builds momentum and keeps you motivated.*

Next up is I

I STANDS FOR INTEREST.

Reflect on your life from ages 5 to 10. Can you remember what brought you joy and engagement? As you transitioned into your teenage years and then stepped into adulthood, what passions persisted? Is there a common thread that reveals parts of you that you haven't fully explored yet?

1. What do you enjoy doing?

Take time to think about the activities that make you feel alive.

2. What are the activities and hobbies you love the MOST?

Consider what you would do in your free time if financial constraints weren't a factor.

3. Do you prefer to lead, follow, or observe when engaging in activities?

Your natural inclination can reveal insights into your role preferences.

4. How do you contribute?

Reflect on the ways you bring value to others. Are you a problem-solver, a supporter, or an innovator?

5. What fascinates you?

Identify the subjects or activities that captivate your attention and spark your curiosity.

6. What did you dream of being when you were a child?

Revisiting childhood aspirations can illuminate your true passions.

7. The SHAPE Formula:

To provide a structured way of understanding yourself, consider the SHAPE formula:

- S: Specific Gifts / Special Gifts

What unique talents or abilities do you possess that set you apart?

- H: Heart

"Where your heart is, there will your treasures be." What causes or activities resonate with your emotions and passions?

- A: Abilities / Skills

What skills have you developed? These could be technical or interpersonal abilities that contribute to your effectiveness.

- P: Personality

What is your personality type? Understanding whether you are more introverted or extroverted, analytical or intuitive can help you find environments where you thrive.

- E: Experience

Consider the experiences you've accumulated throughout your life—both successes and failures. What lessons have you learned, and how have they shaped you?

By excavating your interests and evaluating your SHAPE, you will begin to forge a clearer path to align your life with your passions and purpose. This journey of self-discovery is essential to uncovering the fulfilling experiences that await you. I also stand for another mission-critical word. Integrity.

I STANDS FOR INTEGRITY

Integrity is imperative, especially in the context of living a purposeful life guided by a clear vision. It serves as the foundation for trust, authenticity, and long-term success. Here's why integrity matters and how you can know if you. have it:

Why Integrity is Imperative?

1. Builds Trust

 - Integrity is the cornerstone of trust in relationships, whether personal or professional.

 - When people know you're honest and reliable, they're more likely to support and collaborate with you.

2. Align actions with Values

 - Integrity ensures that your actions align with your core values and vision.

 - Without integrity, it's easy to lose sight of your purpose and make decisions that contradict your beliefs.

3. Fosters Self-Respect

- Living with integrity means being true to yourself, which builds self-esteem and confidence.

- You can look in the mirror and feel proud of who you are and how you've lived.

4. Creates Consistency

- Integrity ensures that your behavior is consistent, even when no one is watching.

- This consistency makes you dependable and predictable in a positive way.

5. Enhances Resilience

- When you act with integrity, you're less likely to be swayed by external pressures or temptations.

- This inner strength helps you stay focused on your vision, even during challenges.

6. Leads to Long-Term Success

- Integrity builds a strong reputation, which opens doors to opportunities.

- People are drawn to those who are honest, ethical, and principled.

How to Know If You Have Integrity

Integrity isn't about being perfect—it's about striving to do the right thing, even when it's hard. Here are some signs that you have integrity:

1. You Keep Your Promises

- If you say you'll do something, you follow through, even if it's inconvenient.

- Example: Showing up on time for a meeting or completing a task you committed to.

2. You're Honest, Even When It's Difficult

- You tell the truth, even if it might lead to discomfort or conflict.

- Example: Admitting a mistake at work instead of covering it up.

3. You Treat Everyone with Respect

- You show kindness and fairness to everyone, regardless of their status or background.

- Example: Listening to someone's opinion, even if you disagree.

4. You Take Responsibility for Your Actions

- You own up to your mistakes and work to make things right.

- Example: Apologizing sincerely and taking steps to avoid repeating the error.

5. You Stand Up for What You Believe In

- You don't compromise your values, even under pressure.

- Example: Refusing to participate in unethical behavior, even if it means losing out on an opportunity.

6. You're Consistent in Your Behaviour

- Your actions align with your words, and you behave the same way whether someone is watching or not.

- Example: Being kind to a stranger, even when no one is around to see it.

7. You Prioritize Doing the Right Thing Over Personal Gain

- You make decisions based on principles, not just what's convenient or beneficial for you.

- Example: Returning a lost wallet instead of keeping the money.

8. You Reflect on Your Actions

- You regularly evaluate whether your behaviour aligns with your values.

- Example: Journaling about your day and asking, Did I act with integrity today?

How to Cultivate Integrity

If you feel like you're falling short in some areas, don't worry—integrity is a skill you can develop. Here's how:

1. Clarify Your Values

- Write down your core values and use them as a guide for decision-making.

- Example: If honesty is a value, commit to telling the truth in all situations.

2. Practice Self-Awareness

- Pay attention to your thoughts, feelings, and actions.

- Ask yourself, Am I being true to my values right now?

3. Set Boundaries

- Know your limits and stick to them, even when it's tempting to compromise.

- Example: Saying no to a request that conflicts with your principles.

4. Seek Feedback

- Ask trusted friends, family, or colleagues if they see you as someone with integrity.

- Be open to constructive criticism and use it to grow.

5. Learn from Mistakes

- When you fall short, acknowledge it, apologize if necessary, and commit to doing better next time.

- Example: If you lied to avoid conflict, reflect on how you can handle similar situations with honesty in the future.

6. Surround Yourself with People of Integrity

- Spend time with individuals who embody the values you admire.

- Their influence can inspire and reinforce your commitment to integrity

Example of Integrity in Action

Imagine you're working on a team project, and a teammate suggests taking credit for someone else's idea to impress the boss. If you have integrity, you might:

- Speak up and say, "That's not right. We should give credit where it's due."

- Suggest an alternative, like acknowledging the original contributor and building on their idea.

- Stand firm, even if it means facing resistance from the team.

Final Thought

Integrity is the glue that holds your vision together. It ensures that your journey toward your goals is not only successful but also meaningful and authentic. By practicing integrity, you build a life of trust, respect, and purpose—one that aligns with your deepest values and inspires others to do the same. Let me know if you'd like more examples or strategies to strengthen your integrity!

As you continue this exploration, keep in mind that your interests, strengths, and values will guide you toward opportunities that invigorate your spirit and lead you to your ultimate Destiny. Remember, this is an evolving process, so be open to what you might discover along the way.

I STANDS FOR INSPIRATION.

Inspiration can come from various sources and manifest differently for everyone.

How to Get Inspired

1. Stay Curious

 - Ask questions, explore new topics, and seek out knowledge.

 - Curiosity opens your mind to new ideas and perspectives.

2. Surround Yourself with Inspiring People

 - Spend time with individuals who motivate and challenge you.

 - Listen to their stories, learn from their experiences, and share your own.

3. Step Out of Your Comfort Zone

 - Try new activities, visit new places, or take on challenges.

 - Growth often happens when you push boundaries.

67

4. Consume Inspiring Content

- Read books, watch documentaries, or listen to podcasts that align with your interests.

- Look for stories of Resilience, innovation, and creativity.

5. Reflect on Your Values and Passions

- Reconnect with what matters most to you. - Ask yourself, What excites me? What do I want to contribute to the world?

6. Practice Mindfulness

- Slow down and pay attention to the present moment.

- Inspiration often strikes when you're calm and open to new ideas.

7. Set Goals and Visualize Success

- Imagine yourself achieving your dreams.

- Visualization can spark motivation and creativity.

8. Engage in Creative Activities

- Write, draw, paint, or play music.

- Creative expression can unlock new ideas and perspectives.

9. Spend Time in Nature

- Nature has a way of calming the mind and sparking inspiration.

- Take a walk, hike, or simply sit outside and observe.

10. Help Others

- Acts of kindness and service can inspire you by reminding you of the impact you can have.

- Volunteer, mentor, or simply lend a listening ear.

Where to Get Inspiration From

1. Books and Literature

- Read biographies, self-help books, or fiction that resonates with you.

- Example: The Alchemist by Paulo Coelho for pursuing dreams.

2. Art and Creativity

- Visit museums and galleries or explore online art platforms.

- Art can evoke emotions and spark new ideas.

3. Music

- Listen to songs that uplift or move you.

- Music has the power to inspire and energize.

4. Nature

- Observe the beauty and complexity of the natural world.

- Nature often provides metaphors for life and growth.

5. Role Models

- Study the lives of people you admire (e.g., entrepreneurs, activists, artists).

- Learn how they overcame challenges and achieved success.

6. Travel and Exploration

- Experience new cultures, landscapes, and ways of life.

- Travel broadens your perspective and inspires creativity.

7. Personal Experiences

- Reflect on your own journey, including challenges and triumphs.

- Your story can be a source of inspiration for yourself and others.

8. Quotes and Affirmations

- Collect quotes that resonate with you and revisit them often.

- Example: "The only way to do great work is to love what you do." – Steve Jobs.

More quotations here….

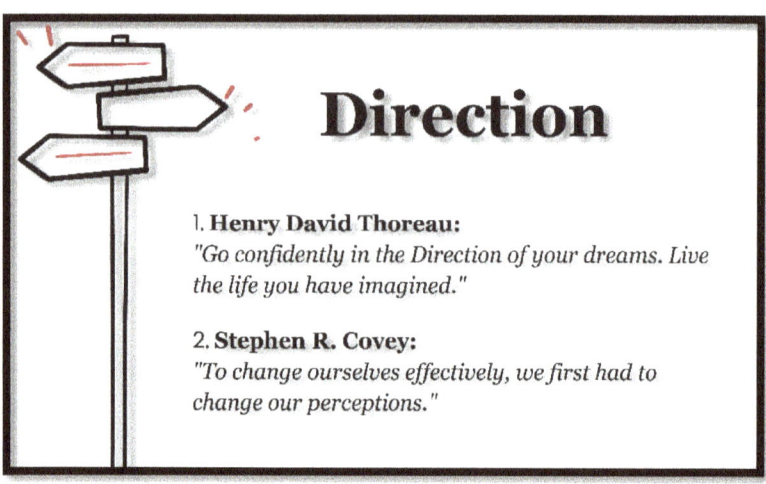

Direction

1. Henry David Thoreau:
"Go confidently in the Direction of your dreams. Live the life you have imagined."

2. Stephen R. Covey:
"To change ourselves effectively, we first had to change our perceptions."

Resilience

1. Maya Angelou:
"You may encounter many defeats, but you must not be defeated. In fact, it may be necessary to encounter defeat, so you can know who you are, what you can rise from, how you can still come out of it."

2. J.K. Rowling:
"Rock bottom became the solid foundation on which I rebuilt my life."

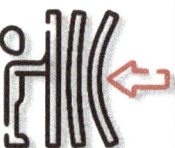

Inspiration

1. Albert Einstein:
"Strive not to be a success, but rather to be of value."

2. Ralph Waldo Emerson:
"What lies behind us and what lies before us are tiny matters compared to what lies within us."

Values

1. Mahatma Gandhi:
"You must be the change you wish to see in the world."

2. C.S. Lewis:
"Integrity is doing the right thing, even when no one is watching."

Empathy

1. Harper Lee:
"You never really understand a person until you consider things from his point of view... Until you climb inside of his skin and walk around in it."

2. Mister Rogers:
"There's no person in the whole world like you, and I like you just the way you are."

9. Community and Collaboration

- Join groups or communities that share your interests.

- Collaboration often leads to new ideas and inspiration.

10. Media and Stories

- Watch inspiring movies, TED Talks, or documentaries.

- Example: The Pursuit of Happiness for perseverance and hope.

Daily Habits to Stay Inspired:

1 **Morning Routine:**
Start your day with something uplifting, like reading a quote or listening to a motivational podcast.

2 **Journaling:**
Write about what inspires you and how you can incorporate it into your life.

3 **Gratitude Practice:**
Reflect on the things that inspire gratitude and joy.

4 **Limit Negativity:**
Reduce exposure to negative news or toxic influences.

5 **Stay Active:**
Physical activity boosts energy and creativity.

Inspiration is everywhere—it's about staying open, curious, and proactive in seeking it out. What inspires you? Let me know if you'd like help exploring specific areas!

Life experiences, both significant and subtle, can serve as profound sources of inspiration. Overcoming challenges or reflecting on pivotal moments like Covid 19 often leads to greater insights and the motivation to pursue one's passions. Meaningful conversations with friends, mentors, or even strangers can ignite inspiration. Sharing ideas and hearing different viewpoints can broaden one's horizons and lead to innovative thinking.

The next letter is V for VALUES.

V STANDS FOR VALUES

Understanding what truly matters to you is integral to aligning your life with your core beliefs and aspirations. To facilitate this process, we can use tools like value cards that help identify and prioritize your core values.

Who Are You?

Take a moment to reflect on your identity. What shapes you? What principles guide your decisions?

What Do You Do?

Consider not only your current job but also your passions and how you contribute to the world around you.

Where Do You Want to Go in Life?

Define your vision for the future. What goals do you aspire to achieve?

To aid in this exploration, I encourage you to take advantage of the value cards available. These cards represent various values, such as honesty, respect, creativity, family, and achievement. By sorting through these cards, you can clarify which values resonate most strongly with you—helping to align your actions with what you deem significant in life. Here is a simple version.

Here are 10 words for each of the key values, along with specific questions to help you reflect on them: THIS IS HOW YOU DO THIS EXERCISE. THIS IS CRUCIAL. PLEASE BE AS HONEST AS POSSIBLE.

1. *Under each word category, choose five words that you most likely identify with.*
2. *Circle the five words for every category.*
3. *You will have 50 words by the time you are done. Do you have your 50 words?*
4. *Now, from each category, pick the one that you most identify with. When you get to the end, you should have only 10 words.*
5. *That will be your CORE VALUES.*
6. *NOW ANSWER THE QUESTIONS AS HONEST AS POSSIBLE.*

Integrity Words:

		Honesty		
	Trustworthiness		Authenticity	
	Transparency	Reliability	Accountability	
Ethics	Principle	Consistency		Sincerity

Questions:

- Do I keep my promises, even when it's inconvenient?

- Am I honest in my words and actions, even when no one is watching?

- Do I admit my mistakes and take responsibility for them?

- Am I consistent in aligning my actions with my beliefs?

- Do I act with sincerity, even when it's difficult?

-2. Empathy

Words:

Questions:

- Am I actively listening to others without judgment?

- Do I try to understand perspectives that are different from my own?

- How often do I offer support or comfort to someone in need?

- Am I patient with others' struggles or mistakes?

- Do I show compassion even when it's not reciprocated?

3. Respect

Words:

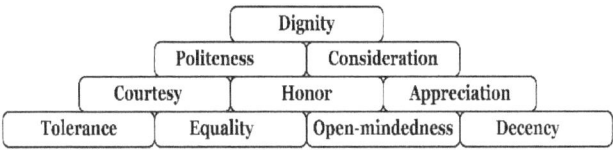

Questions:

- Do I treat everyone with dignity, regardless of their background or opinions?

- Am I mindful of how my words and actions affect others?

- Do I honor boundaries set by others?

- Do I show appreciation for others' contributions?

- Am I open-minded when encountering differing viewpoints?

4. Gratitude

Words:

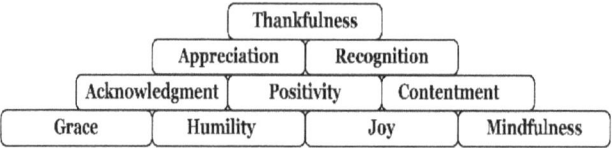

Questions:

- Do I regularly acknowledge the good things in my life?

- How often do I express appreciation to others?

- Am I focusing on what I have rather than what I lack?

- Do I take time to reflect on the positive aspects of my day?

- Am I mindful of the efforts others make for me?

5. Courage

Words:

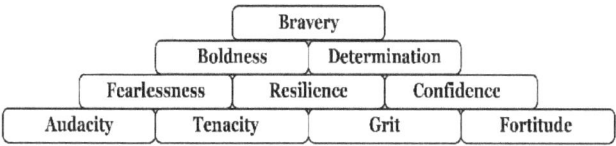

Questions:

- Do I speak up for what I believe in, even when it's uncomfortable?

- Am I willing to take risks to pursue my goals or stand up for others?

- How do I handle fear or uncertainty?

- Do I persevere in the face of challenges?

- Am I bold in pursuing what matters to me?

6. Kindness

Words:

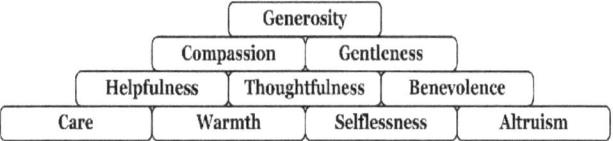

Questions:

- Do I look for opportunities to help others, even in small ways?

- Am I patient and compassionate, even when I'm stressed or busy?

- How often do I perform acts of kindness without expecting anything in return?

- Do I treat others with gentleness and care?

- Am I thoughtful in my interactions with others?

7. Accountability

Words:

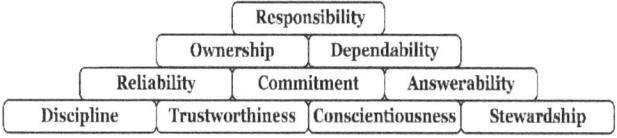

Questions:

- Do I take ownership of my actions and their consequences?

- Am I proactive in fixing my mistakes?

- Do I follow through on commitments, even when it's challenging?

- Am I dependable in my responsibilities?

- Do I hold myself to high standards of discipline?

8. Humility

Words:

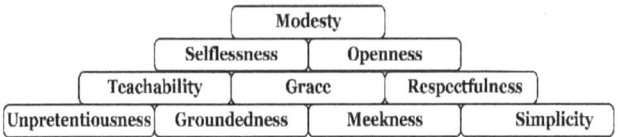

Questions:

- Am I open to feedback and willing to learn from others?

- Do I celebrate others' successes without feeling jealous?

- How do I handle situations where I'm wrong or don't know the answer?

- Am I modest about my achievements?

- Do I approach life with a sense of groundedness and simplicity?

9. Resilience

Words:

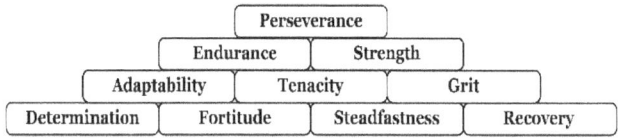

Questions:

- How do I respond to setbacks or failures?

- Am I able to stay focused on my goals despite challenges?

- Do I view obstacles as opportunities to grow?

- Am I adaptable in the face of change?

- Do I bounce back quickly from disappointments?

10. Generosity

Words:

```
                    ┌─────────────┐
                    │    Giving   │
              ┌─────┴──────┬──────┴──────┐
              │ Selflessness │   Charity  │
        ┌─────┴──────┬───────┴────┬───────┴──────┐
        │  Altruism  │ Philanthropy │   Kindness  │
  ┌─────┴─────┬──────┴──────┬──────┴─────┬────────┴──────┐
  │ Liberality │   Sharing   │ Benevolence │ Open-handedness │
  └───────────┴─────────────┴────────────┴─────────────────┘
```

Questions:

- Do I give my time, energy, or resources to others without expecting anything in return?

- Am I willing to share credit or opportunities with others?

- How often do I think about how I can contribute to the well-being of others?

- Do I act with a spirit of charity and goodwill?

- Am I open-handed in my approach to helping others?

These words and questions can serve as a guide to help you reflect on and cultivate each value. Let me know if you'd like further elaboration or additional examples!

Here's an insightful anecdote to illustrate the profound importance of recognizing your intrinsic value:

Imagine a speaker who holds up a $20 bill and asks, "Who wants this $20 bill?" Naturally, nearly all 200 hands go up.

He continues, "I'm going to give this $20 to one of you, but first, let me do this." He crumples the bill in his hands, making it look less appealing.

Then he asks, "Who still wants it?" All hands remain raised.

"Well," he responds, "What if I do this?" He drops the bill on the ground and stomps on it, dirtied and crumpled. He picks it up and shows it to the crowd once more, asking, "Now, who still wants it?"

Once again, every hand goes up.

He concludes, "My friends, I have just shown you a very important lesson. No matter what I did to the money, you still wanted it because its value did not decrease. It was still worth $20.

Many times in life, we find ourselves crumpled, ground down by challenges and poor circumstances. We may make bad decisions that lead us to feel worthless. But remember: no matter what has happened or what will happen, you will never lose your intrinsic value. You are special—don't ever forget it!"

This powerful story serves as a reminder that, like that $20 bill, our value remains unchanged regardless of life's trials.

Embrace your unique qualities and acknowledge that your worth is not defined by your circumstances or the mistakes you make but rather by your core values. Identify what matters most to you, and let those values guide you, helping you stay true to yourself while you pursue your dreams.

Let's take the next step toward understanding how your values influence your decisions and actions. As you connect with your inner self through this exploration, you will find clarity in your path forward.

Core values are the fundamental beliefs you hold about your life. They serve as guiding principles that influence your behaviors, decisions, and actions. These values bring a profound sense of purpose and self-worth, illuminating what matters most to you and what you desire to cultivate in your life.

When you are aware of your core values, you can live in alignment with them. This alignment leads to greater fulfillment, clarity, and self-awareness. Remember, no matter the circumstances you may face, your core values remain steadfast.

Reflect on Your Core Values:

1. Are your values in line with your Heart? Are they congruent?

Take a moment to assess whether your actions and choices align with your values. Misalignment can lead to feelings of dissatisfaction.

2. Which three values are most important to you? Why?

Identify the values that resonate deeply within you. Exploring the reasons behind their significance can offer insights into your priorities.

3. How do your values impact the people around you and what you do?

Think about how your values shape your interactions, relationships, and contributions. Are you uplifting others or reinforcing your beliefs through your actions?

4. Which value is the least important to you? Why?

Understanding the values that hold less significance in your life can help you declutter mental and emotional space for what truly matters.

5. Which value is your MOST motivating factor? Why?

 Recognizing your primary motivating value will help you understand the driving force behind your aspirations and decisions.

6. How will these values help you to reach your Destiny— not just your destination?

 Your core values will act as your compass, guiding you toward meaningful accomplishments that align with your passions and purpose. Reflect on how adhering to these values can facilitate your journey to fulfilling your Destiny.

Practice TAP

To further instill your core values into your daily life, I encourage you to engage in the practice of TAP, which stands for:

-T: Thoughts

Begin each day with positive and intentional thoughts that reflect your core values. Set affirmations to reinforce what you believe in and aspire to be.

- A: Actions

Take deliberate actions that align with your values. This could mean engaging in activities that resonate with your principles, whether that's through your work, community involvement, or personal relationships.

- P: Perceptions

Cultivate a perception of yourself and others that is rooted in your values. Approach situations with empathy and understanding, reflecting the beliefs that guide you.

By regularly practicing TAP, you will ensure that your thoughts, actions, and perceptions are congruent with your core values. This practice will lead you to a more fulfilling, purpose-driven life, helping you navigate the journey toward your ultimate Destiny with confidence.

TAP serves as a reminder to stay true to yourself and your values throughout this transformative journey.

V ALSO STANDS FOR VISION.

Having a vision or a mental picture of your desired future is a powerful tool for providing Direction and purpose in life. It acts as a compass, guiding your decisions, actions, and priorities. Here's how you can create and use a vision as a guiding force.

1. Define Your Vision

A vision is a clear, compelling picture of what you want your future to look like. It should align with your values, passions, and aspirations.

Steps to Define Your Vision:

Reflect on Your Values: What matters most to you? (e.g., family, creativity, impact, health). Refer to your earlier exercise on the page so and so.

- Imagine Your Ideal Life: Close your eyes and visualize where you want to be in 5, 10, or 20 years.

- What does your career look like?

- What kind of relationships do you have?

- How do you spend your time?

- What impact do you want to have on the world?

- Write It Down: Describe your vision in detail. Be specific about what you want to achieve and experience.

Example Vision: "I see myself as a successful entrepreneur running a sustainable business that empowers communities. I have a balanced life, spending quality time with my family, traveling, and contributing to causes I care about. I feel fulfilled, energized, and proud of the impact I'm making."

2. Make Your Vision a Guiding Force

Once you have a clear vision, use it to guide your daily actions and decisions. Here's how:

a. Provide Direction

-Set Goals: Break your vision into long-term and short-term goals.

*- **Example:** If your vision includes running a business, set goals like "Complete a business plan by the end of the year."*

- Prioritize Actions: Focus on activities that move you closer to your vision.

- Ask yourself, "Does this align with my vision?" before committing to tasks or projects.

b. Create Purpose

- Connect Daily Tasks to Your Vision: Even small actions can contribute to your bigger picture.

- *Example:* *If your vision includes better health, daily exercise becomes meaningful because it supports your long-term well-being.*

-Stay Motivated: Remind yourself why your vision matters.

- *Example:* *"I'm building this business to create opportunities for others and leave a legacy."*

3. Use Tools to Keep Your Vision Alive

A vision is only effective if you keep it at the forefront of your mind. Here are some tools to help:

a. Vision Board

- Create a visual representation of your vision using images, quotes, and symbols.

- Place it somewhere you'll see it daily (e.g., your desk or bedroom wall).

b. Journaling

- Write about your vision regularly. Reflect on your progress and adjust as needed.

- Example: "Today, I took a step toward my vision by networking with like-minded professionals."

c. Affirmations

- Use positive statements to reinforce your vision.

- Example: "I am capable of achieving my dreams and living a purposeful life."

d. Visualization

- Spend a few minutes each day imagining yourself living your vision.

- Picture the details: how it looks, feels, and sounds.

-4. Overcome Challenges

Staying focused on your vision isn't always easy. Here's how to navigate obstacles:

a. Stay Flexible

- Life is unpredictable. Be open to adjusting your vision as you grow and learn.

*- **Example:** If your career path changes, adapt your vision to reflect new opportunities.*

b. Build Resilience

- When setbacks occur, remind yourself of your vision and why it matters.

*- **Example:** "This challenge is temporary. I'm working toward something bigger."*

c. Seek Support

- Share your vision with trusted friends, family, or mentors.

- They can offer encouragement, advice, and accountability.

-5. Examples of Vision in Action

Example 1: Career Vision

- *Vision: "I want to be a leader in my industry, known for innovation and integrity."*

- *Guiding Actions:*

- *Pursue advanced training or certifications.*

- *Network with industry leaders.*

- *Take on projects that showcase your skills and values.*

Example 2: Personal Vision

- *Vision: "I want to live a healthy, balanced life filled with meaningful relationships and adventures."*

- *Guiding Actions:*

- *Prioritize self-care (e.g., exercise, meditation).*

- *Spend quality time with loved ones.*

- *Plan trips or experiences that bring joy.*

- Vision: *"I want to create a nonprofit that supports education for underprivileged children."*

- Guiding Actions:

- Research and connect with existing organizations.

- Volunteer or fundraise to gain experience.

- Develop a plan to launch your nonprofit.

6. Benefits of Having a Vision

-Clarity: *You know where you're headed and why.*

-Motivation: *Your vision inspires you to take action, even when things get tough.*

-Focus: *You can prioritize what truly matters and avoid distractions.*

-Resilience: *A strong vision helps you bounce back from setbacks.*

-Fulfilment: *Living in alignment with your vision brings a sense of purpose and satisfaction.*

Final Thought

Your vision is like a lighthouse—it shines a light on your path, even in the darkest times. By defining it, staying connected to it, and taking consistent action, you can turn your mental picture into reality.

Vision" refers to the ability to see the world around you using your eyes, but in a broader sense, it also describes a mental picture of your desired future, acting as a guiding force in your life by providing Direction and purpose, helping you set goals and make decisions to achieve them; essentially, it's what you aspire to become or accomplish, making it crucial for personal growth and motivation.

THE LAST LETTER, E, FOR ELIGIBILITY

Now, let's delve into the last letter, E, which stands for Eligibility. Consider where you currently stand in relation to your goals—both in terms of who you are and what you aspire to accomplish.

1. Where do you stand now?

Reflect on your present circumstances and evaluate how they align with your desired outcomes.

2. What will it take for you to get there?

Identify the steps, resources, and support you need to bridge the gap between where you are and where you want to be.

3. What needs to change in terms of your attitude and behavior?

Are there limiting beliefs or habits that are holding you back? Change often begins with self-reflection and a willingness to adopt a growth mindset.

4. Do you feel you have the potential to be and to do?

Acknowledge your strengths and abilities. Do you believe in your capacity to achieve your dreams?

5. How are you going to demonstrate what you learn?

Commit to putting your insights into action. How will you showcase your growth and newfound knowledge in your daily life?

6. How does this whole experience compare to your past record?

Reflect on your history. How do your current efforts differ from past endeavors? What lessons have you learned? In other words, identify the GAP between your current state and what you want in the future. An acronym here might be helpful. It's called G.R.O.W.

The acronym GROW, commonly used in coaching and mentoring, stands for Goal, Reality, Options, and Will (or Way Forward).

Here's a more detailed explanation:

- *Goal:*

The first step is to define the desired outcome or objective.

- *Reality:*

The second step involves exploring the current situation and identifying any obstacles or challenges.

- *Options:*

The third step focuses on brainstorming potential solutions and strategies to overcome the identified challenges.

- *Will (or Way Forward):*

The final step involves committing to specific actions and outlining a plan to achieve the goal.

Now that you have driven this far, I hope that you are beginning to see the pieces coming together. But of course, we cannot leave without considering one of the most important words that connect everything together.

E ALSO STANDS FOR EMPATHY

Empathy involves not only understanding others but also striving to help them lead fulfilling lives. When you commit to supporting those around you, the outcomes can be transformative:

The Empathy Effect: Seeing, Hearing, and Healing the Human Connection.

"In a world that often confuses empathy with weakness, The Empathy Effect stands as a beacon of courage. This book is not just a guide—it's a revolution. Jeremiah Chin masterfully weaves science, story, and soul into a roadmap for reclaiming our humanity. Whether you're a CEO, a parent, or a weary soul scrolling through life, these pages will remind you: Connection is why we're here."

No man is an island.

Because we are born to connect.

The Empathy Paradox

We live in an age of hyper-connectivity, yet loneliness is an epidemic. We have 500 "friends" online but no one to sit with us in silence during grief. Empathy—the act of stepping into another's shoes without losing ourselves—is the antidote.

This book is not about becoming a saint. It's about practical, everyday bravery:

- Listening so deeply that others feel seen.

- Dissolving the assumptions that divide us.

- Turning empathy into action—in boardrooms, at dinner tables, and in the quiet moments that define us.

What Empathy Is (And What It Isn't)

The ICU Diaries: My personal story.

I kept a deep mental note during the COVID-19 pandemic because it was an unfortunate and unusual event. It was also a time when my mother was gravely ill.

"Patient Mom died today. No family allowed. I held her hand and, hummed a hymn, and offered a silent prayer. I realized this could be her last moment. I sat beside the hospital bed with a live video recording so my family and relatives could watch my mom from their homes. I squeezed her fingers for the last time. Then she was gone. I cried quietly. Not because I didn't love her, but because she died alone. Covid 19 accentuated our powerlessness to connect appropriately."

Seeing my mom's final moments—was empathy in its purest form. Not pity, not problem-solving. Just presence.

And this is how this book is borne.

The Three Faces of Empathy

1. Cognitive Empathy:

Understanding: another's perspective.

Example: Your coworker snaps at you. Instead of retaliating, you think.

"They've been quiet since their mom's passing. Maybe they're overwhelmed." You assume.

2. Emotional Empathy.

Feeling: what they feel.

- Example: Your friend sobs over a breakup. Your throat tightens; tears well up.

Your dog died, and you cried.

You feel.

3. Compassionate Empathy.

Acting to support.

- Example: Your neighbor's car breaks down. You drive their kids to school.

You lost your job. Your buddy volunteered to help you with your expenses with no strings attached.

You connect

The Sympathy Trap.

Sympathy says: "At least you're not homeless!"

Empathy says: "Losing your home must feel terrifying. How can I help?"

Sympathy distances: empathy connects.

The Science of "Feeling With"

Mirror neurons—the brain cells that fire when we watch someone fall clumsily (making us wince) or laugh (making us smile)—are empathy's biological foundation. But empathy isn't automatic. It requires curiosity: a choice to ask, "What's it like to be you?" or What if I'm In his shoes?

The Art of Listening Without an Agenda.

The CEO Who Stopped Talking.

The head of the sales team was disengaged. Morale was low, turnover high.

A coach gave him a radical assignment: "For one week, ask only questions. Don't ask for solutions."

The Empathy Audit

Exercise

For one day, track your interactions.
Each time someone shares a problem,
note:
• **Did you** listen or interrupt?

• **Did you** judge ("You should've...") or validate ("That sounds hard")?

• **Did you** fix or feel? Try it.

Here's an example:
"I'm really mad with my wife. Always treating me like a maid. Telling me what to do."

Honestly.
What was your response?
What were you tempted to do?

Tan resisted. "I'm the boss—fixing things is my job!" Anyway, he heeded my advice, and he tried.

In a particular meeting, he asked:

- "What's the emotional cost of this situation? (fill in your blank in the situation)

- "What's keeping you up at night?"

Are you concerned about the retrenchment of so many of your colleagues?

The shift was seismic. Eric shared burnout stories. Janet admitted fears of failure. Tan realized: "I'd been hearing replies, not feelings of people."

Why We Suck at Listening

-The Interruption Epidemic

The average person waits just 7 seconds before interrupting.

-The Savior Complex

"I need to fix this!"

Spoiler: Rarely(helpful.)

- Distraction

Phones, to-do lists, and mental rehearsals of our next point.

The 90-Second Rule

Neuroscientist Jill Bolte Taylor found that emotional surges (anger, grief, joy) last just 90 seconds—if we let them pass without judgment.

Most couples understand this rule even without realizing it. A couple can fuss and fight, but they soon make up and carry on in life. Still happily married.

Exercise

Next time someone shares, practice:

1. Silence: Breathe. Don't speak for 90 seconds.

2. Body Language: Nod. Lean towards the person.

3. Reflect: "What I'm hearing is..."

Story: The Power of "Mmm"

A therapist once shared her secret: When clients cry, she says "Mmm" —a sound that means "I'm here. Take your time." No advice, no platitudes. Just a hum of humanity.

Try it. Next time someone vents, replace "Let me tell you what to do" with "Mmm."

The Assumption Trap

"You Must Be the Janitor"

Aru, a Black executive, walked into a boardroom for a meeting. A white colleague glanced at him and said, "The trash is over there."

When Aru replied, "I'm the new CFO," the colleague stammered, "I—I didn't realize…"

It happened again a week later. "Why must I keep proving I belong here?" Aru wondered. His story illustrates how assumptions—often rooted in bias—erode trust and connection.

The Science of Snap Judgments

Our brains make split-second judgments to conserve energy (a survival mechanism called the amygdala hijack). But in modern life, this leads to harmful stereotypes. Examples:

- "Teenagers are lazy."

- "Immigrants are taking jobs."

- "They're angry because they're [insert label]."

Exercise

The Day of Curiosity For 24 hours:

1. Pause: When you feel judgment rising ("Ugh, that driver cut me off!"), stop.

2. Question: "What else could be true?" (Maybe they're rushing to the hospital.)

3. Reflect: Journal how shifting assumptions changes your interactions with the situation.

Walking in Their Shoes

Mothers United:

A Story of Grief and Grace

Lucy Chua, a Chinese, and Aminah Salleh, a Malay, both lost sons to violence—Lucy's son to police, Aminah to gang fight. They met at a vigil, where Lucy initially thought, "Her son wasn't innocent like mine. Aminah thought, "She'll never understand my pain."

But they chose to listen. For months, they shared stories over coffee. Lucy learned Aminah's son dreamed of being a teacher. Aminah learned Lucy's son had struggled with addiction. Together, they founded Mothers United, a nonprofit outfit where grieving parents listen first and blame later.

The Science of Perspective-Taking

Studies show that imagining another's life reduces prejudice. For example, reading a story about a cancer person's struggles increases empathy in readers.

Empathy in Action

Exercise

The Perspective Swap:

1. Partner with someone who opposes your view (e.g., politics, parenting styles).

2. Each argues for the other against for 10 minutes.

3. Debrief: What surprised you?

What felt uncomfortable?

The Bully and the Empathy Circle

CEO Lee noticed interpersonal conflicts spiking in his company. Instead of PIP or reprimanding the persons concerned, he created Empathy Circles: Both parties sat together, answering prompts like:

- "What's one pain you've never shared?"

- "What do you wish people knew about you?"

Why are you feeling this way?

One colleague, Jake, an employee, admitted: "My dad yells that I'm a loser every night. I take it out on others because it's easier than feeling small." The girl he bullied, Sofia, whispered, "My mom's in rehab. I'm scared she'll die."

Interpersonal problems dropped 60% that year.

The Science of the "Helper's High"

Acts of kindness release dopamine, a feel-good chemical. Even small gestures—holding a door, texting a friend—boost mood.

Exercise

The 5-Minute Favour

Each day, do one unsolicited act of empathy:

• Pay for a stranger's coffee.

• Write a thank-you note to a colleague.

• Call a relative and say, "I just wanted to hear your voice."

Track your mood for a week. Notice the ripple effect.

Sustaining Empathy Without Burning Out

The Social Worker's Burnout

Emma Wu, a social worker, spent years absorbing her clients' trauma. Panic attacks began. One night, she collapsed sobbing after a child's custody hearing. Her supervisor told her: "You can't pour from an empty cup. Set boundaries or quit."

Emma learned to say: "I can't hold your pain today, but I'm here to listen." She started some mindful meditation self-care and scheduled "empathy-free" hours. Her clients noticed: "You seem calmer. It helps me trust you."

The Science of Compassion Fatigue

Chronic empathy without boundaries floods the body with cortisol (the stress hormone), leading to burnout. Self-care isn't selfish—it's sustainable.

Exercise

The Empathy Reset

1. Breathe : Inhale for 4 counts, hold for 4, exhale for 6. Repeat for 3 minutes.

2. Affirm : Whisper, "I am enough. I can't fix everything, but I can show up."

3. Release : Visualize handing heavy emotions to the earth or sky.

Conclusion: The Ripple Effect

Empathy is contagious. When you choose curiosity over judgment, you give others permission to do the same. Start small:

- Ask a stranger, "How's your heart today?"

- Replace "You're wrong" with "Tell me more."

As poet Naomi Shihab Nye wrote: "Before you know kindness as the deepest thing inside, you must know sorrow as the other deepest thing."

This word is mission critical as Empathy acts as a "glue" because it connects and strengthens the core elements of your personal, mental, emotional, and spiritual foundation, enabling you to navigate life with greater purpose and understanding. Here's how it ties everything together:

Empathy is like a glue that binds your dreams, resilience, inspiration, integrity, and values together because it fosters deep connections—both with yourself and others—while ensuring these elements are aligned in a meaningful and ethical way. Here's how empathy weaves everything together:

1. Dreams: Empathy helps you dream not just for yourself but for the collective good. It allows you to understand the needs and aspirations of others, shaping your dreams to be more inclusive, compassionate, and impactful. When your dreams are rooted in empathy, they become more purposeful and aligned with the well-being of others.

2. Resilience: Empathy strengthens resilience by helping you see challenges as shared human experiences. When you empathize with others who have overcome adversity, you gain perspective and courage to face your own struggles. It also builds supportive relationships, as people are drawn to those who understand and care for them, creating a network that helps you persevere.

3. Inspiration: Empathy opens your heart to the stories, struggles, and triumphs of others, which can deeply inspire you. It fuels your creativity and motivation by showing you what's possible when people care for one another and work together. This inspiration becomes more meaningful when it's guided by empathy, as it encourages you to act in ways that uplift others.

3.1. Integrity: Empathy and integrity go hand in hand. Empathy helps you understand the impact of your actions on others, while integrity ensures you act in a way that is honest, ethical, and aligned with your values. Together, they create a moral compass that guides you to do the right thing, even when it's difficult because you genuinely care about the consequences of your choices.

4. Values: Empathy is the heart of many core values, such as kindness, compassion, and respect. It helps you live out these values by fostering a deep understanding of others' experiences and perspectives. When empathy is the glue, your values are not just abstract ideas—they become actionable principles that guide how you treat others and navigate the world. In essence, empathy binds these elements together by creating a sense of connection, purpose, and humanity. It ensures that your dreams are compassionate, your resilience is supported by relationships, your inspiration is rooted in care for others, your integrity is guided by ethical consideration, and your values are lived out authentically. Together, empathy and these elements create a cohesive, meaningful, and impactful life.

Appendix: The Empathy Toolkit

1. Scripts for Hard Conversations

- "I'm trying to understand. Can you say more?"

- "It sounds like you're feeling...

2. Empathy Playlist: Songs that embody connection (e.g., "Lean on Me," "Bridge Over Troubled Water").

3. Further Reading: Braving the Wilderness (Brené Brown), The War for Kindness (Jamil Zaki).

AFTERWORD BY THE AUTHOR JEREMIAH CHIN

"Years ago, when I was the Sales Manager, I yelled at one of my sales representatives for messing up. Another one of my colleagues looked at me, paused, then said softly: "Rough day, ah boss?" No judgment. No blame. His empathy disarmed me. I burst into tears. That moment was my aha moment. Empathy isn't about getting it right—it's about showing up and being there. Now that you've shown up today, reading this book shows me you care. Now go walk in somebody's shoes.

ABOUT THE AUTHOR

Meet Jeremiah Chin, a true beacon of excellence and commitment in healthcare. Jeremiah is a Singaporean citizen, ready for his next big challenge as an Independent Strategic Business Consultant focused on touching hearts and shaping lives.

His objective? To preserve and improve lives. Jeremiah's career is a tapestry of high-impact roles and achievements. He was the Oncology Country Sales Manager at Schering Plough, then climbed the ranks to become a Regional Sales and Marketing Manager at Pacific Biosciences. He's also been a Sales Manager at DKSH Ethical, an Oncology

Business Executive at Orient Europharma, and a Senior Product Specialist at Novartis Oncology. Most recently, he served as a Biopharma Account Manager at AMGEN Biopharma. His expertise spans various areas — from oncology and key account management to being a certified professional trainer and motivational speaker in hospitals and corporations. He's the person you call when you need someone who's both a heart communicator and a power connector. Jeremiah's educational background is just as impressive.

He holds a Diploma in Retail Management, a Professional Diploma in Leadership and People Management, and an Advanced Certificate in Learning and Performance. He's also a first-prize winner in the Certified Medical Representative category and has bagged numerous awards for his storytelling and service professionalism.

What sets Jeremiah apart is his commitment to lifelong learning and action skills. He's an accredited DISC Training Provider, a Certified Professional Trainer, and a Master Practitioner in public speaking and presentation. He also excelled in customer service as a Certified Service Professional. Jeremiah's career is underpinned by three key attributes- Personality, Passion, and Perseverance.

From a newbie in 1989 to a stalwart in 2024, his journey is a testament to his relentless pursuit of excellence. He's been headhunted by multiple companies thanks to his consistent, result-oriented performance and inspiring team spirit. His rapport with oncologists and hematologists is legendary. It's no wonder he was chosen to head the Oncology Division as Country Sales Manager for Singapore and Malaysia from 1999 to 2001. In 2013, he won the prestigious SHINE Award, which stands for Spirited, Humility, Inspiring, Nurturing, and Enthusiasm. With over three decades of experience, Jeremiah has honed his skills in sales, marketing, training, and leadership. He understands customer needs intimately, both internally and externally. His ability to consistently deliver outstanding performance is a silent testimony to his expertise.

Jeremiah is now looking forward to his next chapter as an Independent Business Consultant after 7 years at Amgen as a Biopharmaceutical Account Manager and 12 months in Juniper Biologics as a Business Manager for ASIA. He is eager to continue making a positive impact wherever he goes. So, if you're looking for someone who embodies excellence, dedication, and a genuine desire to improve lives, Jeremiah Chin is your go-to person. Here's to many more years of strategic consulting excellence.

If you found Jeremiah's journey as inspiring as mine, feel free to reach out to him directly.

www.jeremiahchin.com

Because he never fails to Aspire To Inspire Till Expire.

This course balances theory, self-reflection, and practical exercises to help participants embody empathy in any situation. Perhaps I would like to include this testimony from a healthcare company after attending my workshop with her sales team. Quote:

''We had the pleasure of hosting Jeremiah for a training session with our sales team, and the results were great. His insights into sales strategies, motivation, and mindset truly resonated with our team. The session was not only engaging but also practical, providing actionable takeaways that our team could apply immediately. Thanks to Jeremiah, we saw an increase in energy and confidence among our reps. I highly recommend Jeremiah to any sales organization looking to elevate their team!''

 Jolene Lee, Managing Director AMSCO Healthcare

- You will enjoy a peaceful mind, knowing that you are contributing positively to the lives of others.

- You will cultivate a compassionate Heart that resonates with the experiences of those around you.

- You will develop a willing hand, ready to make the world a better place for everyone.

As we move forward together, I will work with you— Head, Heart, and Hand. I aspire to inspire until I expire.

Now, consider the energy and enthusiasm you bring to your journey.

- Do you have the ENERGY and the ENTHUSIASM to carry your Drive?

 A positive mindset and abundant energy will propel you forward.

- Do you need a coach or mentor to drive beside you?

 It's essential to recognize the value of support on your journey.

- Will you accept me as your Heart and Health MENTOR?

 I'm here to walk alongside you, offering guidance and encouragement.

What Is a Mentor?

A mentor is more than just a guide; he is an experienced and trusted adviser. A mentor:

- Shares valuable insights and wisdom from their experiences.

- Informs about potential paths and challenges you might face.

- Inspires you to push beyond your limits and realize your potential.

- Motivates you through hard times and celebrates your achievements.

- Guides you along your journey, becoming a role model for you to emulate.

In essence, a mentor acts as a consultant, a counselor, and a cheerleader. He stands by your side, helping you navigate the complexities of your path, enabling you to achieve your goals and fulfill your Destiny.

As you embark on this journey, remember that you do not have to walk this path alone. Together, we will cultivate your

135

drive, align your values, embrace your interests, and empower your journey towards a fulfilling life.

CONCLUSION

As the book concludes, you are reminded that your Destiny is a continuous journey, not merely a destination. By embracing the principles of DRIVE, you can navigate challenges with Resilience and inspire those around you on their paths.

With clarity and confidence, individuals are empowered to chart their unique routes, leading to lives filled with passion, purpose, and fulfillment.

DRIVE Your Destiny serves as both a guide and a source of inspiration, inviting readers to embark on a profound journey of self-discovery and growth—one that ultimately leads them toward their true Destiny.

Here is your 30-day challenge thrown in as a bonus for your perseverance.

THANK YOU

YOUR HEART AND HEALTH MENTOR

30 DAYS CHALLENGE ON DRIVE.

For this section, I have chosen DRIVE to stand for

- D - Direction

- R - Resilience

- I - Integrity

- V - Vision

- E - Empathy

It is my hope that this 30-Day DRIVE Challenge will help you cultivate these values and integrate them into your daily life.

01

WEEK 1: DIRECTION

FOCUS: BUILD MENTAL STRENGTH AND ADAPTABILITY. DAILY ACTIONS:

1. Day 1-2: Reflect on your core values. Write down 3-5 values that matter most to you.

2. Day 3-4: Define your short-term and long-term goals. Make sure they align with your values.

3. Day 5-6: Break down one big goal into smaller, actionable steps.

4. Day 7: Create a daily routine that supports your Direction (e.g., morning reflection, planning your day).

02

WEEK 2: RESILIENCE

FOCUS: CLARIFY YOUR PURPOSE AND SET MEANINGFUL GOALS. DAILY ACTIONS:

1. Day 8-9: Identify a recent setback. Write down 3 lessons you learned from it.

2. Day 10-11: Practice gratitude by listing 3 things you're thankful for each day.

3. Day 12-13: Do something outside your comfort zone (e.g., try a new activity, have a difficult conversation).

4. Day 14: Reflect on your progress. Write about how you've grown stronger this week.

139

WEEK 3: INTEGRITY

FOCUS: ALIGN YOUR ACTIONS
WITH YOUR VALUES.
DAILY ACTIONS:

1. Day 15-16: Identify one area where your actions don't fully align with your values. Plan how to improve.

2. Day 17-18: Practice honesty in all your interactions, even in small ways.

3. Day 19-20: Take responsibility for a mistake and make amends if needed.

4. Day 21: Reflect on how living with integrity has impacted your relationships and self-respect.

WEEK 4: VISION

FOCUS: STAY FOCUSED ON YOUR
LONG-TERM PURPOSE.
DAILY ACTIONS:

1. Day 22-23: Visualize your ideal future. Write or draw what it looks like.

2. Day 24-25: Review your goals and adjust them if necessary. Ensure they still align with your vision.

3. Day 26-27: Take one step toward a long-term goal (e.g., research, plan, or start a project).

4. Day 28: Reflect on how your vision inspires and motivates you.

FINAL DAYS: EMPATHY

FOCUS: STRENGTHEN YOUR CONNECTIONS WITH OTHERS. DAILY ACTIONS:

1. Day 29: Practice active listening. Have a conversation where you focus entirely on the other person.

2. Day 30: Perform an act of kindness without expecting anything in return (e.g., help a stranger, write a thank-you note).

3. Bonus Reflection: Write about how practicing empathy has enriched your relationships and perspective.

141

TIPS FOR SUCCESS

- Journal Daily: Spend 5-10 minutes each day reflecting on your progress and insights.

- Celebrate Wins: Acknowledge your achievements, no matter how small.

- Stay Flexible: If you miss a day, don't stress—just pick up where you left off.

By the end of the 30 days, you'll have a stronger sense of Direction, greater Resilience, deeper Integrity, a clearer Vision, and more Empathy.

Acknowledgement:

"I can do all things through Christ who strengthens me." Philippians 4:13

www.ingramcontent.com/pod-product-compliance
Lightning Source LLC
Chambersburg PA
CBHW050442150626
46551CB00028B/1116